This library edition published in 2012 by Walter Foster Publishing, Inc.
Distributed by Black Rabbit Books.
P.O. Box 3263 Mankato, Minnesota 56002

Designed and published by Walter Foster Publishing, Inc.
Walter Foster is a registered trademark.

Printed in Mankato, Minnesota, USA by CG Book Printers, a division of Corporate Graphics.

First Library Edition

Library of Congress Cataloging-in-Publication Data

Watch me draw Cinderella's enchanted world / illustrated by Marianne
Tucker ; colored by José Maria Cardona ; step-by-step drawing
illustrations by Elizabeth T. Gilbert. -- First Library Edition.
      pages cm
  ISBN 978-1-936309-86-3
  1. Cartoon characters--Juvenile literature. 2.
Drawing--Technique--Juvenile literature. 3. Cinderella (Legendary
character)--Juvenile literature. I. Tucker, Marianne, illustrator. II.
Gilbert, Elizabeth T., illustrator. III. Walt Disney Enterprises.
  NC1764.W374 2012
  741.5'1--dc23
                                    2012005299

052012
17679

9 8 7 6 5 4 3 2 1

Watch Me Draw
Cinderella's
Enchanted World

Illustrated by Marianne Tucker

Colored by José Maria Cardona

Step-by-Step Drawing Illustrations by Elizabeth T. Gilbert

A dream is a wish the heart makes—and friends help make those dreams come true!

Draw the mouse!

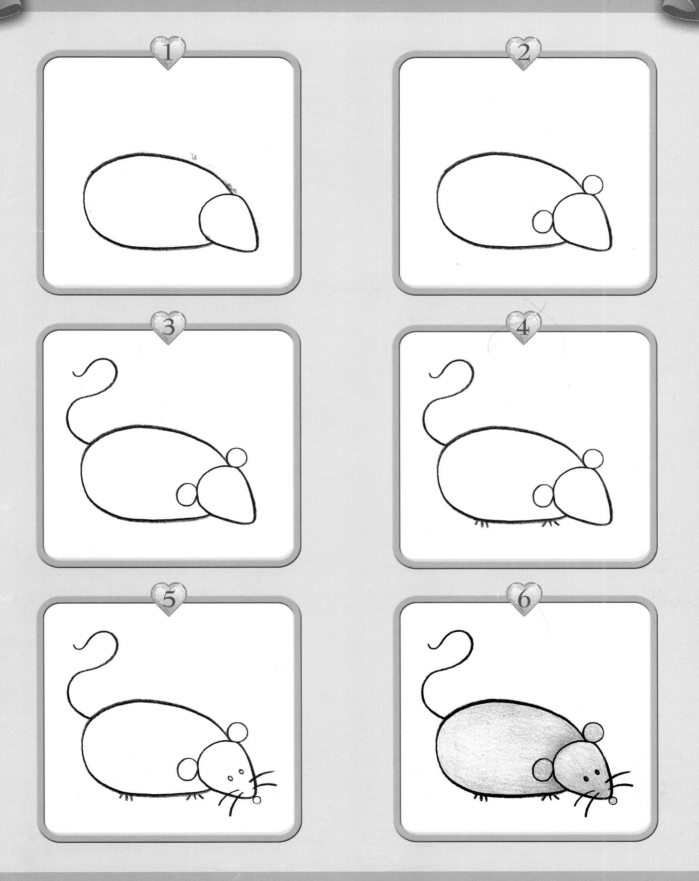

Magic is all about timing, but
"once upon a time" can happen anytime.

Draw the clock!

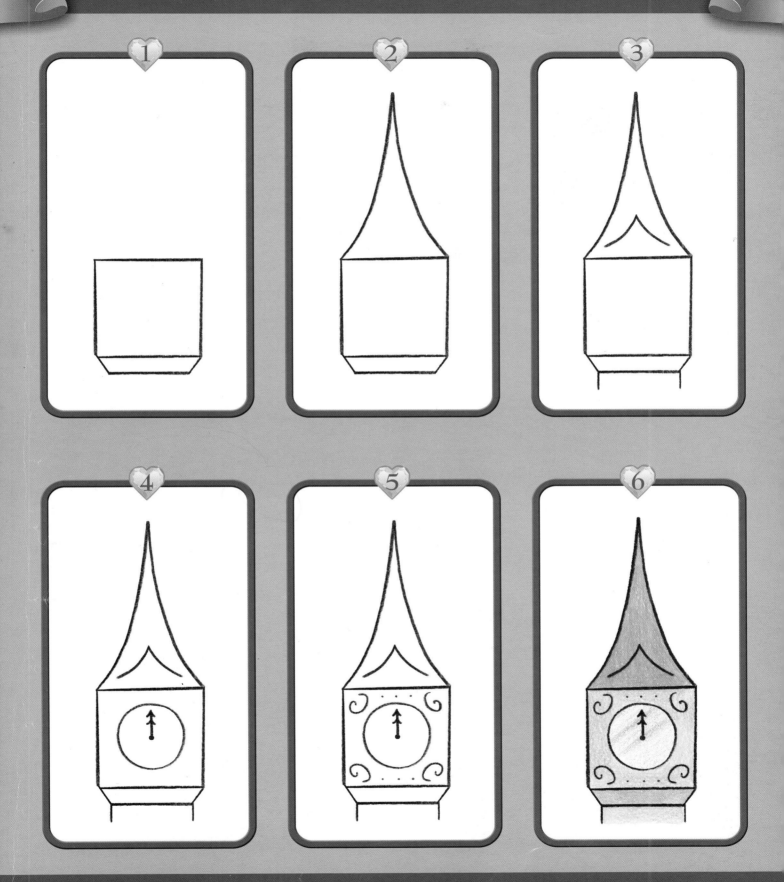

Thanks to her fairy godmother, Cinderella went from scullery maid to princess.

Draw the ball gown!

When you dare to believe, the ordinary can become extraordinary!

Draw the coach!

Not every princess is born into royalty. But if the shoe fits . . .

Draw the glass slipper!

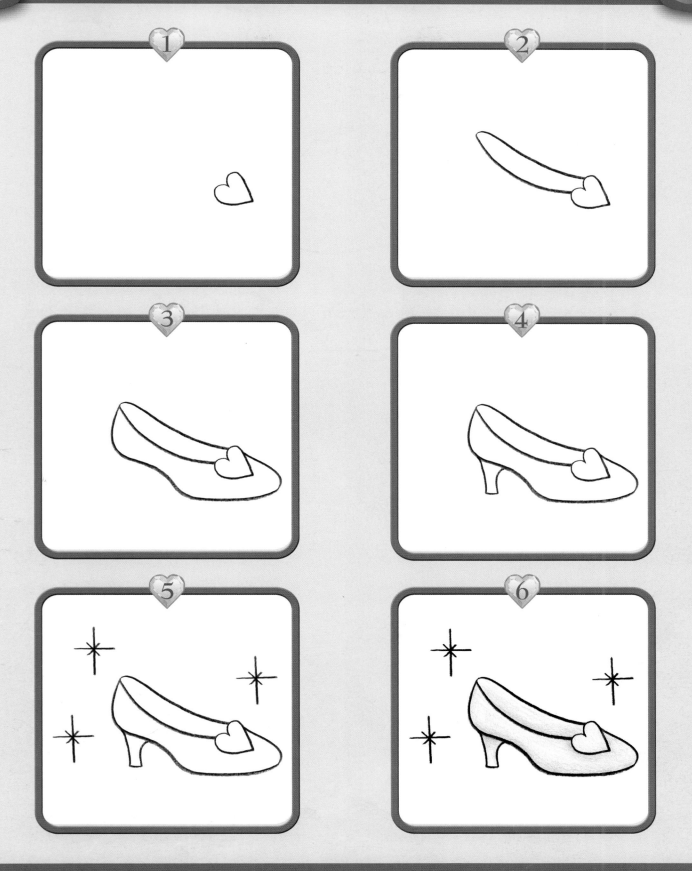

The loveliest of mornings can interrupt the most beautiful of dreams!

Draw the bird!

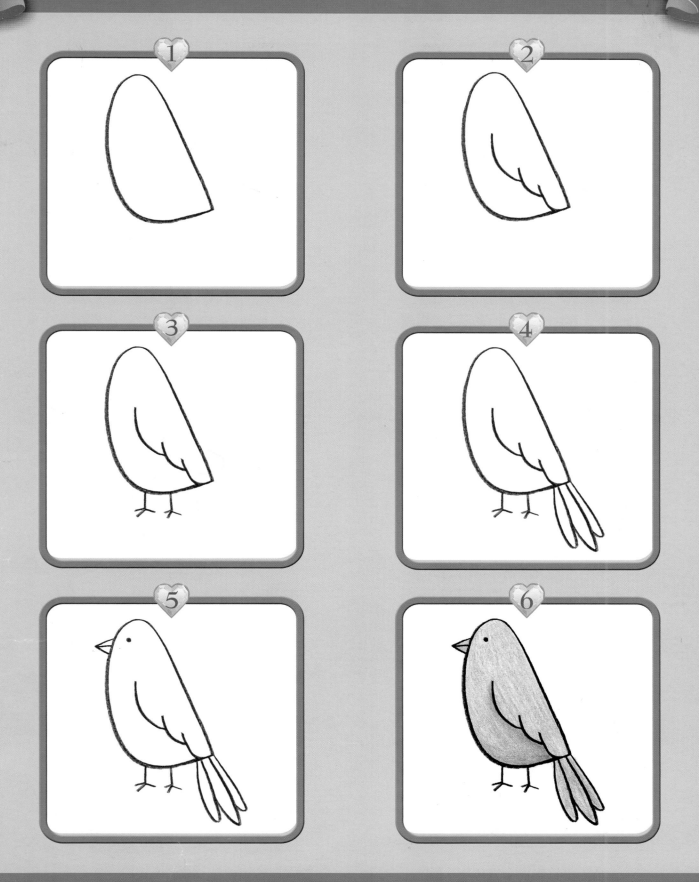

When the heart rings true,
there's reason to celebrate!

Draw the bell!

Tiaras and gowns are beautiful,
but it's love that makes a girl want to twirl!

Draw the tiara!

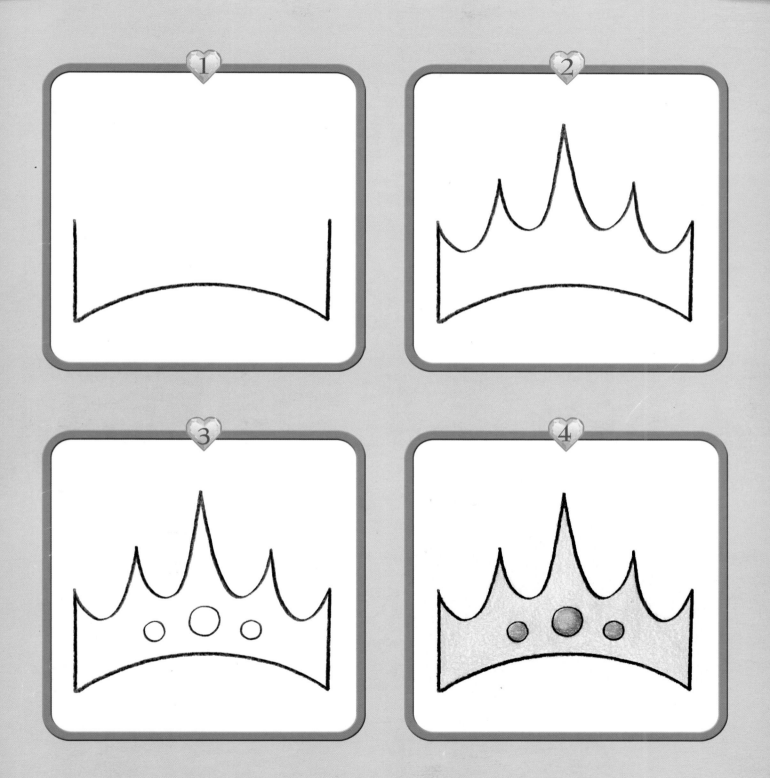

With a "Bibbidi-Bobbidi-Boo!"
a white horse can appear out of the blue!

Draw the horse!

A happy heart makes the most beautiful music.

Draw the trumpet!

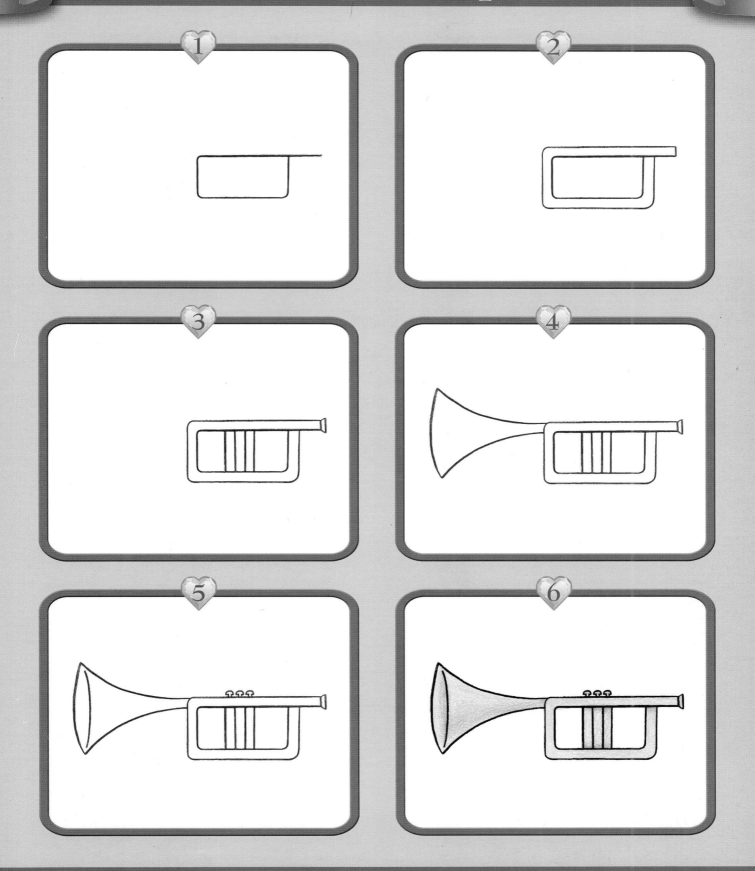

It's true that home is where the heart is—and for Cinderella, home is with the Prince in the royal palace!

Draw the palace!

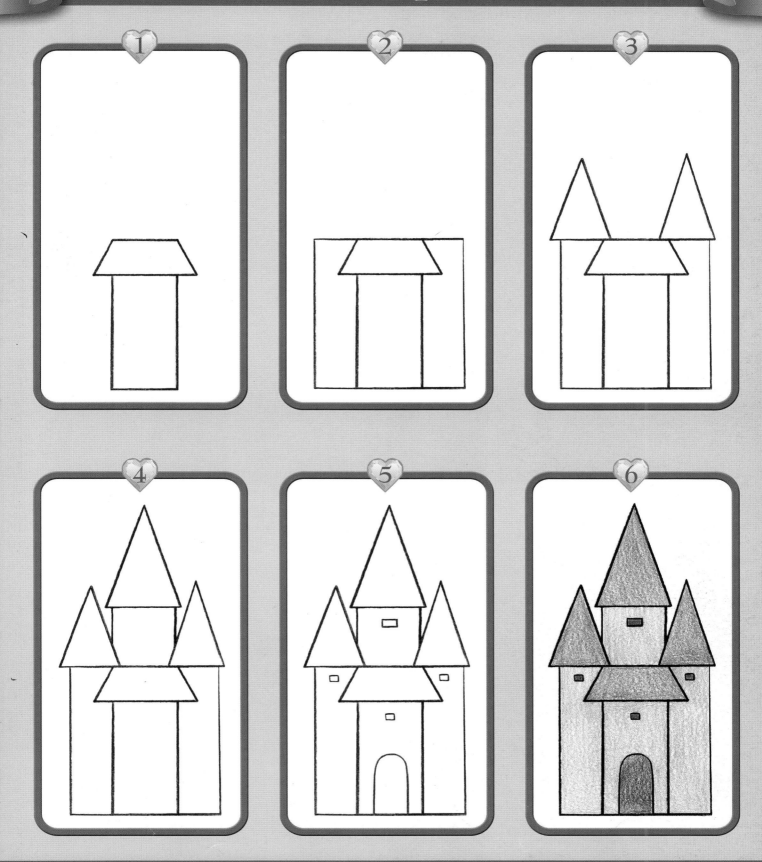

If you believe, even the most wonderful dreams can come true!